This journal belongs to

....

YOU ARE A BELOVED CHILD OF GOD,
precious to Him in every way. As you seek Him,
He will show you the mysteries of life and unfold His
unique plans for you—a life full of rich blessing.

God cares about you and knows all the desires of your heart.
He is as close as breathing. Let this journal inspire you
to express your thoughts, record your prayers,
embrace your loving Shepherd,
and listen for His voice calling you.

May His goodness and mercy
follow you all the days of your life.

One thing God has spoken, two things have I heard:
that you, O God, are strong, and that you, O Lord, are loving.
PSALM 62:11–12 NIV†

The Lord Is My Shepherd

Promise Journal

Ellie Claire™
gift & paper expressions

...inspired by life

The King of love my Shepherd is,
Whose goodness faileth never;
I nothing lack if I am His,
And He is mine forever.

SIR HENRY WILLIAMS BAKER

THE LORD IS
MY SHEPHERD;
I SHALL NOT WANT.

GOD'S CONSTANT CARE

The LORD is my shepherd; I shall not want.
He maketh me to lie down in green pastures:
he leadeth me beside the still waters.
He restoreth my soul:
he leadeth me in the paths of righteousness
for his name's sake.
Yea, though I walk through
the valley of the shadow of death,
I will fear no evil:
for thou art with me;
thy rod and thy staff they comfort me.
Thou preparest a table before me
in the presence of mine enemies:
thou anointest my head with oil;
my cup runneth over. Surely goodness and
mercy shall follow me all the days of my life:
and I will dwell in the house of the LORD for ever.

PSALM 23:1–6 KJV

God is the shepherd in search of His lamb.
His legs are scratched, His feet are sore,
and His eyes are burning. He scales the cliffs
and traverses the fields. He explores the caves.
He cups His hands to His mouth and calls into the canyon.
And the name He calls is yours.

MAX LUCADO

God never abandons anyone on whom He has set His love;
nor does Christ, the good shepherd, ever lose track of His sheep.

J. I. PACKER

Every Need

God wants nothing from us except our needs, and these
furnish Him with room to display His bounty
when He supplies them freely.... Not what I have,
but what I do not have, is the first point of contact
between my soul and God.

CHARLES H. SPURGEON

God is not only the answer to a thousand needs,
He is the answer to a thousand wants. He is
the fulfillment of our chief desire in all of life.
For whether or not we've ever recognized it,
what we desire is unfailing love. Oh, God,
awake our souls to see—You are what we want,
not just what we need.
Yes, our life's protection,
but also our heart's affection.

BETH MOORE

Jesus Christ has brought every need, every joy,
every gratitude, every hope of ours before God.
He accompanies us and brings us into the presence of God.

DIETRICH BONHOEFFER

Just as there comes a warm sunbeam
into every cottage window, so comes a love—
born of God's care for every separate need.

NATHANIEL HAWTHORNE

My God is changeless in his love for me, and he will come and help me.

PSALM 59:10 TLB

God of All Comfort

You are never alone. In your heart of hearts,
in the place where no two people are ever alike,
Christ is waiting for you. And what
you never dared hope for springs to life.

BROTHER ROGER OF TAIZÉ

God comforts. He doesn't pity. He picks us up, dries our tears,
soothes our fears, and lifts our thoughts beyond the hurt.

ROBERT SCHULLER

God walks with us.... He scoops us up in His arms
or simply sits with us in silent strength until
we cannot avoid the awesome recognition
that yes, even now, He is here.

GLORIA GAITHER

And when the storm is passed, the brightness
for which He is preparing us will shine out unclouded,
and it will be Himself.

MORROW COFFEY GRAHAM

There may be times in your life when it all seems dark
and you cannot see or trace the hand of God,
but yet God is working. Just as much as He works in
the bright sunlight, He works all through the night.

The LORD is near to the brokenhearted and saves those who are crushed in spirit.

PSALM 34:18 NASB

HELD IN HIS HAND

The mystery of life is that the Lord of life
cannot be known except in and through the act of living.
Without the concrete and specific involvements of
daily life we cannot come to know the loving presence
of Him who holds us in the palm of His hand....
Therefore, we are called each day
to present to our Lord the whole of our lives.

HENRI J. M. NOUWEN

God promises to keep us in the palm of His hand,
with or without our awareness. God has already made a
space for us, even if we have not made a space for God.

DAVID AND BARBARA SORENSEN

Faith allows us to continually delight in life since
we have placed our needs in God's hands.

JANET L. SMITH

That Hand which bears all nature up
Shall guard His children well.

WILLIAM COWPER

The impetus of God's love comes from within Himself,
to share with us His life and love. It is a beautiful,
eternal gift, held out to us in the hands of love.
All we have to do is say "Yes!"

JOHN POWELL

Behold, I have inscribed you on the palms of My hands.

ISAIAH 49:16 NASB

LOVER OF MY SOUL

Solitude is a place inside myself where
God's Spirit and my spirit dwell together in union.
This place within me is private and reserved
for the intimacies that God and I share.
What happens between the two of us in that place
is not meant for public consumption.
It is a place where I can give myself with abandon
to the Lover of my soul.

RUTH HALEY BARTON

If you are seeking after God, you may be sure of this:
God is seeking you much more. He is the Lover,
and you are His beloved. He has promised Himself to you.

JOHN OF THE CROSS

Time passed in silence with God is time spent
growing in relationship with Him.
And time spent letting His love flow through
you to others is an investment in eternity.

AMY AND JUDGE REINHOLD

You are in the Beloved...therefore infinitely
dear to the Father, unspeakably precious to Him.
You are never, not for one second, alone.

NORMAN DOWTY

The LORD is righteous in all his ways and loving toward all he has made.
The LORD is near to all who call on him, to all who call on him in truth.

PSALM 145:17–18 NIV†

The Rhythm of God

From the heart of God comes the strongest rhythm—
the rhythm of love. Without His love reverberating in us,
whatever we do will come across like a noisy gong
or a clanging symbol. And so the work of the human heart,
it seems to me, is to listen for that music
and pick up on its rhythms.

KEN GIRE

Like art, like music, like so many other disciplines,
prayer can only be appreciated when you
actually spend time in it. Spending time with the Master
will elevate your thinking. The more you pray,
the more will be revealed. You will appreciate not only
the greatness of prayer, but the greatness of God.

JONI EARECKSON TADA

Life is what we are alive to. It is not length but breadth....
Be alive to...goodness, kindness, purity, love, history, poetry, music,
flowers, stars, God, and eternal hope.

MALTBIE D. BABCOCK

Nothing can give you quite the same thrill
as the feeling that you are in harmony with the great
God of the universe who created all things.

DR. JAMES DOBSON

Sing songs to the tune of his glory, set glory to the rhythms of his praise.

PSALM 66:2 MSG

SHEPHERD AND GUARDIAN

I am the good shepherd. I know my own and my own know me,
just as the Father knows me and I know the Father;
and I lay down my life for the sheep.

JOHN 10:14–15 ESV

He tends his flock like a shepherd:
he gathers the lambs in his arms
and carries them close to his heart;
he gently leads those that have young.

ISAIAH 40:11 NIV

All we like sheep have gone astray;
we have turned every one to his own way;
and the LORD hath laid on him the iniquity of us all.

ISAIAH 53:6 KJV

You were continually straying like sheep,
but now you have returned to the Shepherd
and Guardian of your souls.

1 PETER 2:25 NASB

Come, let us bow down in worship,
let us kneel before the LORD our Maker;
for He is our God
and we are the people of His pasture,
the flock under His care.

PSALM 95:6–7 NIV

Genuine love sees faces, not a mass: the Good Shepherd calls His own sheep by name.

GEORGE A. BUTTRICK

Walking with God

My Lord God, I have no idea where I am going.
I do not see the road ahead of me. I cannot
know for certain where it will end....
But I believe that the desire to please You
does in fact please You. And I hope
I have that desire in all that I am doing.
I hope that I will never do anything apart
from that desire. And I know that if I do this,
You will lead me by the right road
though I may know nothing about it.

Therefore will I trust You always,
though I may seem to be lost
and in the shadow of death.
I will not fear, for You are ever with me.
And You will never leave me
to face my perils alone.

Thomas Merton

God gets down on His knees among us;
gets on our level and shares Himself with us.
He does not reside afar off and send
diplomatic messages, He kneels among us....
God shares Himself generously and graciously.

Eugene Peterson

Yet I am always with you; you hold me by my right hand.

PSALM 73:23 NIV

You Matter to Him

The God who created, names,
and numbers the stars in the heavens also
numbers the hairs of my head.... He pays attention
to very big things and to very small ones.
What matters to me matters to Him,
and that changes my life.

ELISABETH ELLIOT

What matters supremely is not the fact that
I know God, but the larger fact which underlies it—
the fact that He knows me. I am graven on
the palms of His hands. I am never out of His mind.
All my knowledge of Him depends
on His sustained initiative in knowing me.
I know Him because He first knew me,
and continues to know me.

J. I. PACKER

One hundred years from today
your present income will be inconsequential.
One hundred years from now
it won't matter if you got that big break....
It will greatly matter that you knew God.

DAVID SHIBLEY

I'm not saying that I have this all together, that I have it made.
But I am well on my way, reaching out for Christ,
who has so wondrously reached out for me.

PHILIPPIANS 3:12 MSG

GOD WANTS YOU

Listening to God is a firsthand experience....
God invites *you* to vacation in His splendor.
He invites *you* to feel the touch of His hand.
He invites *you* to feast at His table.
He wants to spend time with *you*.

MAX LUCADO

The Most High calls to us and waits for us to respond.
He desires to quench our deepest thirst,
to satisfy our deepest hunger, and to fill us
with His power and presence as we dwell
in the secret place of the Most High.

CYNTHIA HEALD

He is a God who can be found.
A God who can be known. A God
who wants to be close to us.
That's why He is called Immanuel,
which means "God with us." But He
draws close to us as we draw close to Him.

STORMIE OMARTIAN

I want you woven into a tapestry of love,
in touch with everything there is to know of God.
Then you will have minds confident and at rest,
focused on Christ, God's great mystery.

COLOSSIANS 2:2 MSG

*God's hand is always there; once you grasp it
you'll never want to let it go.*

His Faithful Care

God takes care of His own. He knows our needs.
He anticipates our crises. He is moved by our weaknesses.
He stands ready to come to our rescue.
And at just the right moment He steps in
and proves Himself as our faithful heavenly Father.

CHARLES SWINDOLL

We are of such value to God that He
came to live among us...and to guide us home.
He will go to any length to seek us,
even to being lifted high upon the cross
to draw us back to Himself. We can only respond
by loving God for His love.

CATHERINE OF SIENNA

I know that God is faithful. I know that He answers prayers,
many times in ways I may not understand.

SHEILA WALSH

If you believe in God, it is not too difficult
to believe that He is concerned about the universe
and all the events on this earth. But the really
staggering message of the Bible is that
this same God cares deeply about you
and your identity and the events of your life.

BRUCE LARSON

Your unfailing love is as high as the heavens.
Your faithfulness reaches to the clouds.

PSALM 57:10 NLT

God Is Great

The simple fact of being...in the presence of the Lord
and of showing Him all that I think, feel, sense,
and experience, without trying to hide anything,
must please Him. Somehow, somewhere,
I know that He loves me, even though I do not
feel that love as I can feel a human embrace,
even though I do not hear a voice as I hear
human words of consolation.... God is greater
than my senses, greater than my thoughts,
greater than my heart.
I do believe that He touches me in places
that are unknown even to myself.

HENRI J. M. NOUWEN

Have you ever thought what a wonderful
privilege it is that everyone each day
and each hour of the day has the liberty
of asking God to meet him in the inner chamber
and to hear what He has to say?

ANDREW MURRAY

The LORD your God is with you....
He will take great delight in you,
he will quiet you with his love,
he will rejoice over you with singing.

ZEPHANIAH 3:17 NIV[†]

God is the sunshine that warms us, the rain that melts the frost and waters the young plants. The presence of God is a climate of strong and bracing love, always there.

JOAN ARNOLD

Like the summer breezes playing,
like the tall trees softly swaying,
like the lips of silent praying
is the perfect peace of God.

MICHAEL PERRY

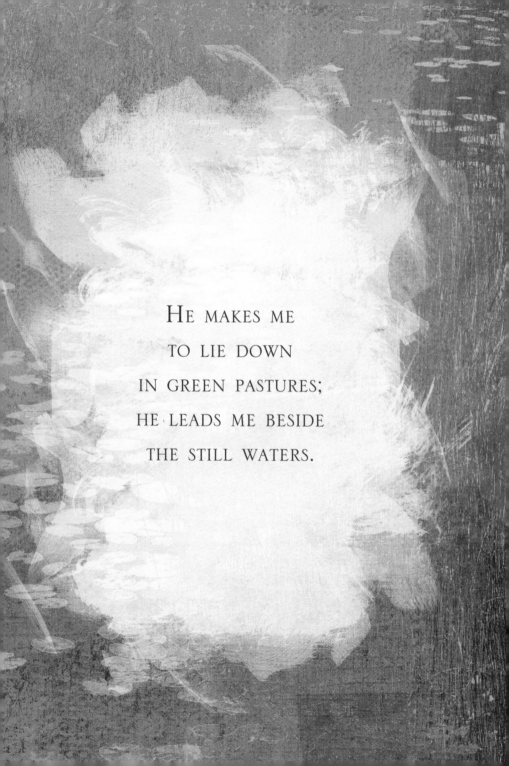

HE MAKES ME
TO LIE DOWN
IN GREEN PASTURES;
HE·LEADS ME BESIDE
THE STILL WATERS.

Enfolded in Peace

I will let God's peace infuse every part of today.
As the chaos swirls and life's demands pull at me on all sides,
I will breathe in God's peace that surpasses all understanding.
He has promised that He would set within me
a peace too deeply planted to be affected by
unexpected or exhausting demands.

Calm me, O Lord, as You stilled the storm,
Still me, O Lord, keep me from harm.
Let all the tumult within me cease,
Enfold me, Lord, in Your peace.

Celtic Traditional

Only God gives true peace—a quiet gift
He sets within us just when we think
we've exhausted our search for it.

How much greater is my peace when
I find it has come in the midst of the storm
and not because He stilled its forces.

Leita Twyeffort

God cannot give us a happiness and peace apart from Himself,
because it is not there. There is no such thing.

C. S. Lewis

God's peace...is far more wonderful than the human mind can understand.
His peace will keep your thoughts and your hearts quiet and at rest.

PHILIPPIANS 4:7 TLB

DRINK DEEPLY

We must drink deeply from the very Source
the deep calm and peace of interior quietude
and refreshment of God, allowing the pure water
of divine grace to flow plentifully
and unceasingly from the Source itself.

MOTHER TERESA

I pray that God, the source of hope,
will fill you completely with joy and peace
because you trust in Him. Then you will
overflow with confident hope through
the power of the Holy Spirit.

ROMANS 15:13 NLT

He is the Source. Of everything.
Strength for your day.
Wisdom for your task. Comfort for your soul.
Grace for your battle. Provision for each need.
Understanding for each failure.
Assistance for every encounter.

JACK HAYFORD

In difficulties, I can drink freely
of God's power and experience His touch
of refreshment and blessing—much like
an invigorating early spring rain.

ANABEL GILLHAM

Those who drink the water I give will never be thirsty again. It becomes a fresh, bubbling spring within them, giving them eternal life.

JOHN 4:14 NLT

WAITING QUIETLY

Dear Father, I have so many questions
and so few answers. Reveal to me Your will.
Show me Your path and give me
the wisdom to follow it. Feed me from Your Word,
O Lord, and teach me Your ways.
When the questions of life are confusing
or overwhelming, remind me to wait on You,
the One who has all the answers. Amen.

In waiting we begin to get in touch
with the rhythms of life—stillness and action,
listening and decision. They are the rhythms of God.
It is in the everyday and the commonplace
that we learn patience, acceptance, and contentment.

RICHARD J. FOSTER

Love comes while we rest against our Father's chest.
Joy comes when we catch the rhythms of His heart.
Peace comes when we live in harmony with those rhythms.

KEN GIRE

A quiet morning with a loving God
puts the events of the upcoming day
into proper perspective.

JANETTE OKE

I wait for the LORD, my whole being waits, and in his word I put my hope.
I wait for the Lord more than watchmen wait for the morning.

PSALM 130:5–6 NIV

He Comes in Stillness

He doesn't come in the roaring thunder,
as we expect. He doesn't write in blazing lightning
as it flashes across the clouds, even though
we watch for Him there. His voice won't be
in the rushing wind or in the pounding rhythm
of the waves breaking against the seashore.
He simply comes to us in a still small voice.

WENDY MOORE

We may ask, "Why does God bring
thunderclouds and disasters when we want
green pastures and still waters?" Bit by bit,
we find behind the clouds, the Father's feet;
behind the lightning, an abiding day that has no night;
behind the thunder, a still small voice
that comforts with a comfort that is unspeakable.

OSWALD CHAMBERS

"Go out, and stand on the mountain before the LORD."
And behold, the LORD passed by, and a great
and strong wind tore into the mountains...,
but the LORD was not in the wind;
and after the wind an earthquake,
but the LORD was not in the earthquake;
and after the earthquake a fire, but the LORD
was not in the fire; and after the fire
a still small voice.

1 KINGS 19:11–12

The lightning and thunder, they go and they come,
But the stars and the stillness are always at home.

GEORGE MACDONALD

TAKE TIME

Intimacy may not be rushed.... We can't
dash into God's presence and choke down
spiritual inwardness before we hurry to
our one o'clock appointment.
Inwardness is time-consuming, open only
to minds willing to sample spirituality
in small bites, savoring each one.

CALVIN MILLER

It may seem strange to think that God
wants to spend time with us, but...think about it.
If God went to all the trouble to come to earth,
to live the life that He did, to die for us,
then there's got to be a hunger and a passion behind that.
We think of prayer as an "ought to,"
but in reality it is a response to God's
passionate love for us. We need to refocus
on the fact that God is waiting for us to show up
and be with Him and that our presence
truly touches Him.

DR. HENRY CLOUD

Come and sit and ask Him whatever is on your heart.
No question is too small, no riddle too simple.
He has all the time in the world.
Come and seek the will of God.

MAX LUCADO

I've loved you the way my Father has loved me.
Make yourselves at home in my love.

JOHN 15:9 MSG

Rest in Him

Truly my soul finds rest in God alone;
my salvation comes from him.
Truly he is my rock and my salvation;
he is my fortress, I will never be shaken....
My salvation and my honor depend on God;
he is my mighty rock, my refuge.
Trust in him at all times, O people;
pour out your hearts to him,
for God is our refuge....
One thing God has spoken,
two things have I heard:
that you, O God, are strong,
and that you, O Lord, are loving.

Psalm 62:1–2, 7–8, 11–12 niv[†]

If God gives such attention to the appearance of wildflowers—
most of which are never even seen—don't you think
he'll attend to you, take pride in you, do his best for you?...
Steep your life in God-reality, God-initiative, God-provisions.
Don't worry about missing out. You'll find all
your everyday human concerns will be met.

Matthew 6:30, 33 msg

Rest in the Lord, and wait patiently for Him.

Psalm 37:7

When God finds a soul that rests in Him and is not easily moved...
to this same soul He gives the joy of His presence.

CATHERINE OF GENOA

BEAUTIFUL PEACE

In comparison with this big world, the human heart
is only a small thing. Though the world is so large,
it is utterly unable to satisfy this tiny heart.
Our ever growing soul and its capacities can
be satisfied only in the infinite God.
As water is restless until it reaches its level,
so the soul has no peace until it rests in God.

SADHU SUNDAR SINGH

No one can get inner peace by pouncing on it,
by vigorously willing to have it. Peace is a margin
of power around our daily need.
Peace is a consciousness of springs too deep
for earthly droughts to dry up.

HARRY EMERSON FOSDICK

Out of your relationship with God come life's greatest
treasures—fellowship, wisdom, peacefulness of soul,
eternal hope, gladness of heart, direction and meaning,
and a glorious purpose in all you do.

ROY LESSIN

Drop Thy still dews of quietness
Till all our strivings cease;
Take from our souls the strain and stress,
And let our ordered lives confess
The beauty of Thy peace.

JOHN GREENLEAF WHITTIER

You will keep in perfect peace all who trust in you,
all whose thoughts are fixed on you!

ISAIAH 26:3 NLT

A River of Delights

Your love, O LORD, reaches to the heavens,
your faithfulness to the skies.
Your righteousness is like the mighty mountains,
your justice like the great deep....
How priceless is your unfailing love, O God!
People take refuge in the shadow of your wings.
They feast on the abundance of your house;
you give them drink from your river of delights.
For with you is the fountain of life;
in your light we see light.

PSALM 36:5–9 NIV

From God, great and small, rich and poor,
draw living water from a living spring,
and those who serve Him freely and gladly
will receive grace answering to grace.

THOMAS À KEMPIS

Where your pleasure is, there is your treasure:
where your treasure, there your heart;
where your heart, there your happiness.

AUGUSTINE

Joy is perfect acquiescence in God's will
because the soul delights itself in God Himself.

H. W. WEBB-PEPLOE

God's love is like a river springing up in the
Divine Substance and flowing endlessly through His creation,
filling all things with life and goodness and strength.

THOMAS MERTON

An Invitation

Are you tired? Worn out? Burned out on religion?
Come to me. Get away with me and you'll recover your life.
I'll show you how to take a real rest. Walk with me
and work with me—watch how I do it.
Learn the unforced rhythms of grace. I won't lay
anything heavy or ill-fitting on you.
Keep company with me and you'll
learn to live freely and lightly.

Matthew 11:28–30 MSG

[God] is looking for people who will come
in simple dependence upon His grace,
and rest in simple faith upon His greatness.
At this very moment, He's looking at you.

Jack Hayford

You've always given me breathing room,
a place to get away from it all,
a lifetime pass to your safe-house,
an open invitation as your guest.

Psalm 61:3 MSG

God waits for us in the inner sanctuary of the soul.
He welcomes us there.

Richard J. Foster

Come with me by yourselves to a quiet place and get some rest.

MARK 6:31 NIV

Come to the Water

For I will pour water on the thirsty land,
and streams on the dry ground;
I will pour out my Spirit on your offspring,
and my blessing on your descendants.
They will spring up like grass in a meadow,
like poplar trees by flowing streams.

Isaiah 44:3–4 NIV

Come, all you who are thirsty,
come to the waters;
and you who have no money,
come, buy and eat!
Come, buy wine and milk
without money and without cost.
Why spend money on what is not bread,
and your labor on what does not satisfy?
Listen, listen to me, and eat what is good,
and you will delight in the richest of fare.
Give ear and come to me;
listen, that you may live.
I will make an everlasting covenant with you.

Isaiah 55:1–3 NIV

Is anyone thirsty? Come!
All who will, come and drink,
Drink freely of the Water of Life!

Revelation 22:17 MSG

Jesus knows when a request comes to Him from the heart.
He has been waiting all along for us to bring our needy selves to Him
and receive from Him that eternal water.

DORIS GAILEY

AUDIENCE OF ONE

Solitude liberates us from entanglements
by carving out a space from which we can see ourselves
and our situation before the Audience of One.
Solitude provides the private place where we can
take our bearings and so make God our North Star.

OS GUINNESS

Solitude begins with a time and place for God,
and God alone. If we really believe not only
that God exists but also that He is actively present in our lives—
healing, teaching, guiding—we need to set aside
a time and space to give Him our undivided attention.

HENRI J. M. NOUWEN

Find a quiet, secluded place so you won't
be tempted to role-play before God. Just be there
as simply and honestly as you can manage.
The focus will shift from you to God,
and you will begin to sense his grace....
This is your Father you are dealing with,
and he knows better than you what you need.
With a God like this loving you, you can pray very simply.

MATTHEW 6:6, 8–9 MSG

You have set Your glory above the heavens.
Thy glory flames from sun and star:
Center and soul of every sphere,
yet to each loving heart how near.

OLIVER WENDELL HOLMES

Refreshed and Renewed

Your thoughts—how rare, how beautiful!
God, I'll never comprehend them! I couldn't even begin to
count them—any more than I could count the sand of the sea.
Oh, let me rise in the morning and live always with you!

PSALM 139:17 MSG

When we allow God the privilege of shaping our lives,
we discover new depths of purpose and meaning.
What a joyful thought to realize you
are a chosen vessel for God—
perfectly suited for His use.

JONI EARECKSON TADA

But as for me, I shall sing of Your strength;
Yes, I shall joyfully sing
of Your lovingkindness in the morning,
For You have been my stronghold.

PSALM 59:16 NASB

May our lives be illumined
by the steady radiance
renewed daily,
of a wonder,
the source of which
is beyond reason.

DAG HAMMARSKJÖLD

You're all I want in heaven! You're all I want on earth!...
I'm in the very presence of GOD—oh, how refreshing it is!
I've made Lord GOD my home. GOD, I'm telling the world what you do!

PSALM 73:25, 27–28 MSG

The law of the LORD is perfect, refreshing the soul....
The commands of the LORD are radiant, giving light to the eyes....
The decrees of the LORD are firm, and all of them are righteous.

PSALM 19:7–9 NIV

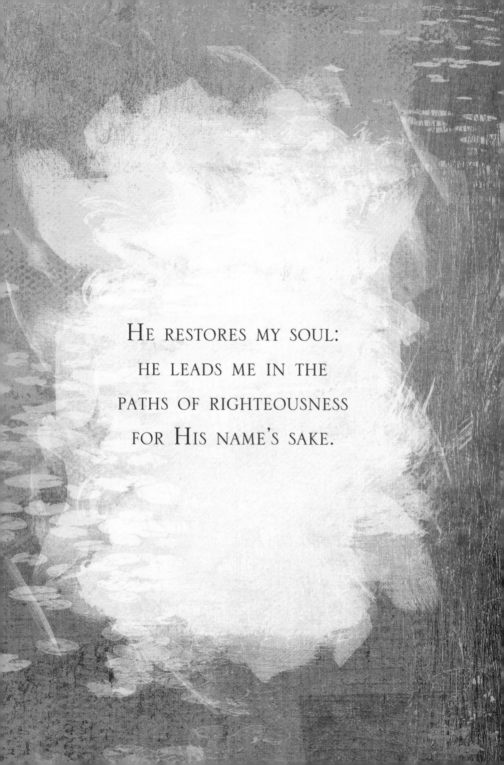

HE RESTORES MY SOUL:
HE LEADS ME IN THE
PATHS OF RIGHTEOUSNESS
FOR HIS NAME'S SAKE.

TO BE ALIVE

To be alive, to be able to see, to walk, to have a home,
music, paintings, friends—it's all a miracle. I have
adopted the technique of living life from miracle to miracle.

ARTUR RUBINSTEIN

When we focus on God, the scene changes.
He's in control of our lives; nothing lies
outside the realm of His redemptive grace.

PENELOPE J. STOKES

There are only two ways to live your life.
One is as though nothing is a miracle.
The other is as though everything is a miracle.

RICHARD CRASHAW

Show me your ways, LORD...
Guide me in your truth and teach me,
for you are God my Savior,
and my hope is in you all day long.
Remember, LORD, your great mercy and love....
According to your love remember me,
for you, LORD, are good.

PSALM 25:4–7 NIV

In the presence of hope—faith is born.
In the presence of faith, love becomes a possibility!
In the presence of love—miracles happen!

ROBERT SCHULLER

I have come that they may have life, and that they may have it more abundantly.

JOHN 10:10

HEART AND SOUL

Whether sixty or sixteen, there is in every human being's heart
the love of wonder, the sweet amazement at the stars
and starlike things, the undaunted challenge of events,
the unfailing childlike appetite for what-next,
and the joy of the game of living.

SAMUEL ULLMAN

Of all earthly music, that which reaches farthest into heaven
is the beating of a truly loving heart.

HENRY WARD BEECHER

I will remember that when I give Him my heart,
God chooses to live within me—
body and soul. He fills all of the empty places,
His very Spirit inside of me.

The meaning of earthly existence lies,
not as we have grown used to thinking, in prospering,
but in the development of the soul.

ALEKSANDR SOLZHENITSYN

Oh, the wild joys of living!
The leaping from rock up to rock....
How good is man's life, the mere living!
How fit to employ
All the heart and the soul
And the senses forever in joy!

ROBERT BROWNING

Dear friend, I pray that you may enjoy good health and that all may go well with you, even as your soul is getting along well.

3 JOHN 1:2 NIV

A Centered Life

Life from the Center is a life of unhurried peace and power.
It is simple. It is serene.... We need not get frantic.
He is at the helm. And when our little day is done,
we lie down quietly in peace, for all is well.

THOMAS R. KELLY

Because we are spiritual beings...it is for our good,
individually and collectively, to live our lives
in interactive dependence upon God.

DALLAS WILLARD

Oh, the depth of the riches both of the wisdom
and knowledge of God! How unsearchable are His
judgments and His ways past finding out!... For of Him
and through Him and to Him are all things,
to whom be glory forever. Amen.

ROMANS 11:33, 36

There is nothing but God's grace.
We walk upon it; we breathe it; we live and die by it;
it makes the nails and axles of the universe.

ROBERT LOUIS STEVENSON

Faith in God gives your life a center from which
you can reach out and dare to love the world.

BARBARA FARMER

For in him we live and move and have our being.

ACTS 17:28 NIV

RESTORATION

Whatever your loss, pain, failure, or brokenness,
Jesus Christ is fully capable of bringing about
change unto full restoration. Just as His
resurrection power brings new life,
His redemption power brings new hope.
He is able, for He's more than a Savior!
He's your Redeemer who promises that He will
give "beauty for ashes, the oil of joy for mourning."

JACK HAYFORD

He has sent me to bind up the brokenhearted,
to proclaim freedom for the captives
and release from darkness for the prisoners...
to bestow on them a crown of beauty instead of ashes,
the oil of joy instead of mourning,
and a garment of praise instead of a spirit of despair.

ISAIAH 61:1, 3 NIV

Whatever He may demand of us, He will give us
at the moment the strength and courage that we need.

FRANÇOIS FÉNELON

Though I walk in the midst of trouble,
You will revive me;
You will stretch forth Your hand...
and Your right hand will save me.

PSALM 138:7 NASB

How calmly may we commit ourselves to the hands of Him who bears up the world.

JEAN PAUL RICHTER

Faithful Guide

God, who has led you safely on so far,
will lead you on to the end. Be altogether
at rest in the loving holy confidence
which you ought to have in His heavenly Providence.

FRANCIS DE SALES

Guidance is a sovereign act. Not merely does God
will to guide us by showing us His way...whatever
mistakes we may make, we shall come safely home.
Slippings and strayings there will be,
no doubt, but the everlasting arms are beneath us;
we shall be caught, rescued, restored.
This is God's promise; this is how good He is.
And our self-distrust, while keeping us humble,
must not cloud the joy with which
we lean on our faithful covenant God.

J. I. PACKER

A new path lies before us;
We're not sure where it leads;
But God goes on before us,
Providing all our needs.
This path, so new, so different
Exciting as we climb,
Will guide us in His perfect will
Until the end of time.

LINDA MAURICE

When we obey him, every path he guides us on is fragrant with his loving-kindness and his truth.

PSALM 25:10 TLB

Be Still and Know

Bestow upon me, O Lord my God,
understanding to know Thee, diligence to seek Thee,
wisdom to find Thee, and a faithfulness
that may finally embrace Thee.

Thomas Aquinas

Perhaps this moment is unclear, but let it be—
even if the next, and many moments after that,
are unclear, let them be. Trust that God will help you
work them out, and that all the unclear moments
will bring you to that moment of clarity
and action when you are known by Him and know Him.
These are the better and brighter moments of His blessing.

Wendy Moore

We must concentrate on knowing God;
the more we know Him the more we want to know Him.
And as knowledge is commonly the measure of love,
the deeper and wider our knowledge,
the greater will be our love.

Brother Lawrence

They who seek the throne of grace
Find that throne in every place;
If we live a life of prayer,
God is present everywhere.

Oliver Holden

Be still, and know that I am God!

PSALM 46:10 NLT

OUR GRACIOUS GOD

The grace of God means something like:
Here is your life. You might never have been, but you *are*
because the party wouldn't have been complete without you.
Here is the world. Beautiful and terrible things will happen.
Don't be afraid. I am with you. Nothing can ever separate us.
It's for you I created the universe. I love you.

FREDERICK BUECHNER

The LORD longs to be gracious to you;
therefore he will rise up to show you compassion.

ISAIAH 30:18 NIV

His overflowing love delights to make us
partakers of the bounties He graciously imparts.

HANNAH MORE

God makes everything come out right;
he puts victims back on their feet....
He doesn't endlessly nag and scold,
nor hold grudges forever.
He doesn't treat us as our sins deserve,
nor pay us back in full for our wrongs.
As high as heaven is over the earth,
so strong is his love to those who fear him.
And as far as sunrise is from sunset,
he has separated us from our sins.

PSALM 103:6, 9–12 MSG

Lord...give me only Your love and Your grace.
With this I am rich enough, and I have no more to ask.

IGNATIUS OF LOYOLA

RENEWED BY HIS BEAUTY

The joyful birds prolong the strain,
their song with every spring renewed;
the air we breathe, and falling rain,
each softly whispers: God is good.

JOHN HAMPDEN GURNEY

All the world is an utterance of the Almighty.
Its countless beauties, its exquisite adaptations,
all speak to you of Him.

PHILLIPS BROOKS

Be still, and in the quiet moments, listen to the voice
of your heavenly Father. His words can renew your spirit...
no one knows you and your needs like He does.

JANET L. SMITH

Lord...give me the gift of faith to be renewed
and shared with others each day.
Teach me to live this moment only, looking neither
to the past with regret, nor the future with apprehension.
Let love be my aim and my life a prayer.

ROSEANN ALEXANDER-ISHAM

Our Creator would never have made such lovely days,
and given us the deep hearts to enjoy them,
above and beyond all thought,
unless we were meant to be immortal.

NATHANIEL HAWTHORNE

Worship the LORD in the beauty of holiness!

PSALM 96:9

OPEN YOUR HEART

The "air" which our souls need also envelops
all of us at all times and on all sides. God is round about us
in Christ on every hand, with many-sided and all-sufficient grace.
All we need to do is to open our hearts.

OLE HALLESBY

Jesus Christ opens wide the doors of the
treasure house of God's promises, and bids us go in
and take with boldness the riches that are ours.

CORRIE TEN BOOM

Life begins each morning.... Each morning
is the open door to a new world—
new vistas, new aims, new tryings.

LEIGH MITCHELL HODGES

Live for today but hold your hands open to tomorrow.
Anticipate the future and its changes with joy.
There is a seed of God's love in every event,
every circumstance, every unpleasant situation
in which you may find yourself.

BARBARA JOHNSON

Everything in life is most fundamentally a gift.
And you receive it best, and you live it best,
by holding it with very open hands.

LEO O'DONOVAN

The steadfast love of the Lord never ceases, his mercies never come to an end;
they are new every morning; great is your faithfulness.

LAMENTATIONS 3:22–23 NRSV

THE SPIRITUAL LIFE

The spiritual life is first of all a life. It is not merely
something to be known and studied, it is to be lived....
We live as spiritual people when we live as people
seeking God. If we are to become spiritual,
we must remain human.

THOMAS MERTON

Prayer is by nature a dialogue between man and God.
It unites the soul with its Creator and reconciles the two.
Its effect is to hold the world together.

JOHN CLIMACUS

I stayed awake all night,
prayerfully pondering your promise....
You're the closest of all to me, GOD,
and all your judgments true.

PSALM 119:148, 151 MSG

God was spirit and He gave man a spirit so that He could
come into Him and mingle His own life with man's life.

MADAME JEANNE GUYON

Prayer is the way the life of God is nourished....
We look upon prayer as a means of getting things
for ourselves; the Bible's idea of prayer is that
we may get to know God Himself.

OSWALD CHAMBERS

The highest pinnacle of the spiritual life is not joy in unbroken sunshine,
but absolute and undoubting trust in the love of God.

A. W. THOROLD

Fresh Hope

God specializes in things fresh and firsthand.
His plans for you this year may outshine those of the past....
He's preparing to fill your days with reasons to give Him praise.

JONI EARECKSON TADA

Hope is not a granted wish or a favor performed;
no, it is far greater than that. It is a zany,
unpredictable dependence on a God
who loves to surprise us out of our socks.

MAX LUCADO

God...rekindles burned-out lives with fresh hope,
restoring dignity and respect to their lives—
a place in the sun! For the very structures
of earth are God's; he has laid out
his operations on a firm foundation.

1 SAMUEL 2:7–8 MSG

How could I be anything but quite happy
if I believed always that all the past is forgiven,
and all the present furnished with power,
and all the future bright with hope.

JAMES SMETHAM

Every day we live is a priceless gift of God,
loaded with possibilities to learn something new,
to gain fresh insights.

DALE EVANS ROGERS

Trust steadily in God, hope unswervingly, love extravagantly.

1 CORINTHIANS 13:13 MSG

Sanctuary of the Soul

Deep within us all there is an amazing inner
sanctuary of the soul, a holy place, a Divine Center,
a speaking Voice, to which we may continuously return.
Eternity is at our hearts, pressing upon our
time-torn lives, warming us with intimations
of an astounding destiny, calling us home unto Itself.
Yielding to these persuasions...utterly and completely,
to the Light within, is the beginning of true life.

Thomas R. Kelly

The soul is like a wild animal—tough, resilient,
resourceful, savvy, self-sufficient. It knows
how to survive in hard places. But it is also shy.
Just like a wild animal, it seeks safety
in the dense underbrush. If we want to see a wild animal,
we know that the last thing we should do
is go crashing through the woods
yelling for it to come out. But if we will
walk quietly into the woods, sit patiently
by the base of the tree, and fade into our surroundings,
the wild animal we seek might put in an appearance.

Parker Palmer

As for God, his way is perfect:
The Lord's word is flawless;
he shields all who take refuge in him.

Psalm 18:30 niv

Within each of us there is an inner place where the
living God Himself longs to dwell, our sacred center of belief.

When all my plans and hopes are fading like a shadow,
When all my dreams lie crumbled at my feet,
I will look up and know the night will bring tomorrow,
And that my Lord will bring me what I need.

GLORIA GAITHER

YEA, THOUGH I WALK
THROUGH THE VALLEY
OF THE SHADOW OF DEATH,
I WILL FEAR NO EVIL:
FOR YOU ARE WITH ME;
YOUR ROD AND YOUR STAFF,
THEY COMFORT ME.

Take Refuge

Let my soul take refuge...beneath the shadow
of Your wings: let my heart, this sea of restless waves,
find peace in You, O God.

AUGUSTINE

You, O LORD, are a shield about me,
my glory, and the lifter of my head.
I cried aloud to the LORD,
and he answered me from his holy hill.

PSALM 3:3–4 ESV

Wait upon God's strengthening, and say to Him,
"O Lord, You have been our refuge in all generations."
Trust in Him who has placed this burden on you.
What you yourself cannot bear,
bear with the help of God who is all-powerful.

BONIFACE

Why would God promise a refuge unless He knew
we would need a place to hide once in a while?

NEVA COYLE

Blessed be the LORD, my rock...he is my steadfast love
and my fortress, my stronghold and my deliverer,
my shield and he in whom I take refuge.

PSALM 144:1–2 ESV

The LORD is good, a refuge in times of trouble.
He cares for those who trust in him.

NAHUM 1:7 NIV

SHINING PROMISES

Our feelings do not affect God's facts.
They may blow up, like clouds, and cover the eternal things
that we do most truly believe. We may not see the shining
of the promises—but they still shine!

AMY CARMICHAEL

Commit to hope. There's reason to! For the believer,
hope is divinely assured things that aren't here yet!
Our hope is grounded in unshakable promises.

JACK HAYFORD

However things may appear to be, of all possible
circumstances—those circumstances in whose midst
I am set—these are the best that He could choose for me.
We do not know how this is true—where would faith be
if we did?—but we do know that all things that happen
are full of shining seed.

This is my Father's world;
He shines in all that's fair.
In the rustling grass I hear Him pass;
He speaks to me everywhere.

MALTBIE D. BABCOCK

God's promises are like the stars;
the darker the night the brighter they shine.

DAVID NICHOLAS

He knows the way I take; when He has tried me,
I shall come forth as gold.

JOB 23:10 NASB

Don't Be Afraid

Don't be afraid, I've redeemed you.
I've called your name. You're mine.
When you're in over your head, I'll be there with you.
When you're in rough waters, you will not go down.
When you're between a rock and a hard place,
it won't be a dead end—because I am God,
your personal God, The Holy of Israel, your Savior.
I paid a huge price for you...! *That's* how much
you mean to me! *That's* how much I love you!

ISAIAH 43:1–4 MSG

God is our refuge and strength,
A very present help in trouble.
Therefore we will not fear,
Even though the earth be removed.

PSALM 46:1–3

Do not be afraid. I am the First and the Last.
I am the Living One; I was dead, and now look,
I am alive for ever and ever!

REVELATION 1:17–18 NIV

If God be for us, who can be against us?

ROMANS 8:31 KJV

Do not be afraid to enter the cloud that is settling down on your life.
God is in it. The other side is radiant with His glory.

L. B. COWMAN

LIMITLESS HOPE

Hope is a state of mind, not of the world. Hope,
in this deep and powerful sense, is not the same as joy
that things are going well, or willingness to invest in enterprises that
are obviously heading for success, but rather an ability
to work for something because it is good.

VACLAV HAVEL

"For I know the plans I have for you," declares the LORD,
"plans to prosper you and not to harm you,
plans to give you hope and a future."

JEREMIAH 29:11 NIV

When life becomes difficult, when cracks spread
through our existence and our strength seems to leak out,
fill the gaps with hope. Like gold adorning distressed ancient art,
hope will reinforce, add value, and reveal more beauty.

BARBARA FARMER

O Lord, you alone are my hope.
I've trusted you, O LORD, from childhood.

PSALM 71:5 NLT

When we take time to notice the simple things in life,
we never lack for encouragement. We discover we are surrounded
by a limitless hope that's just wearing everyday clothes.

Hope is faith holding out its hands in the dark.

GEORGE ILES

Amazing Grace

This is the amazing story of God's grace. God saves us
by His grace and transforms us more and more
into the likeness of His Son by His grace. In all our trials
and afflictions, He sustains and strengthens us by His grace.
He calls us by grace to perform our own unique
function within the Body of Christ. Then, again by grace,
He gives to each of us the spiritual gifts necessary
to fulfill our calling. As we serve Him,
He makes that service acceptable to Himself by grace,
and then rewards us a hundredfold by grace.

Jerry Bridges

God has not promised skies always blue,
flower-strewn pathways all our lives through;
God has not promised sun without rain,
joy without sorrow, peace without pain.
But God has promised strength for the day,
rest for the labor, light for the way,
grace for the trials, help from above,
unfailing sympathy, undying love.

Annie Johnson Flint

After winter comes the summer.
After night comes the dawn. And after every storm,
there comes clear, open skies.

Samuel Rutherford

Behold, God is my helper; the Lord is the sustainer of my soul.

PSALM 54:4 NASB

Totally Aware

God is every moment totally aware of each one of us.
Totally aware in intense concentration and love....
No one passes through any area of life, happy or tragic,
without the attention of God with him.

EUGENIA PRICE

God knows everything about us.
And He cares about everything. Moreover,
He can manage every situation. And He loves us!
Surely this is enough to open the wellsprings of joy....
And joy is always a source of strength.

HANNAH WHITALL SMITH

Because God is responsible for our welfare,
we are told to cast all our care upon Him, for He cares for us.
God says, "I'll take the burden—don't give it a thought—
leave it to Me." God is keenly aware that we are dependent
upon Him for life's necessities.

BILLY GRAHAM

God reads the secrets of the heart. God reads its most
intimate feelings, even those which we are not aware of.

JEAN-NICHOLAS GROU

You are God's created beauty and the focus
of His affection and delight.

JANET L. SMITH

Give all your worries and cares to God, for he cares about you.

1 PETER 5:7 NLT

LIGHT IN THE DARKNESS

There is not enough darkness in all the world to
put out the light of one small candle.... In moments of
discouragement, defeat, or even despair, there are always
certain things to cling to. Little things usually: remembered
laughter, the face of a sleeping child, a tree in the wind—
in fact, any reminder of something deeply felt or dearly loved.

No one is so poor as not to have many of these small candles.
When they are lighted, darkness goes away
and a touch of wonder remains.

ARTHUR GORDON

One taper lights a thousand,
Yet shines as it has shone;
And the humblest light may kindle
A brighter than its own.

HEZEKIAH BUTTERWORTH

I believe that God is in me as the sun is in the color
and fragrance of a flower—the Light in my darkness,
the Voice in my silence.

HELEN KELLER

Into all our lives, in many simple, familiar, homely ways,
God infuses this element of joy from the surprises of life,
which unexpectedly brighten our days,
and fill our eyes with light.

SAMUEL LONGFELLOW

It is you who light my lamp; the LORD my God lightens my darkness.

PSALM 18:28 ESV

GUIDED BY HIS HAND

God guides us, despite our uncertainties and our
vagueness, even through our failings and mistakes....
He leads us step by step, from event to event.
Only afterwards, as we look back over
the way we have come and reconsider certain
important moments in our lives in the light
of all that has followed them, or when
we survey the whole progress of our lives,
do we experience the feeling of having been led
without knowing it, the feeling that God
has mysteriously guided us.

PAUL TOURNIER

When God has become our shepherd, our refuge,
our fortress, then we can reach out to Him
in the midst of a broken world
and feel at home while still on the way.

HENRI J. M. NOUWEN

God's holy beauty comes near you, like a spiritual scent,
and it stirs your drowsing soul.... He creates in you
the desire to find Him and run after Him—
to follow wherever He leads you, and to press
peacefully against His heart wherever He is.

JOHN OF THE CROSS

I'll lead you to buried treasures, secret caches of valuables—
Confirmations that it is, in fact, I, GOD...who calls you by your name.

ISAIAH 45:3 MSG

THE STRONGHOLD

The LORD is the stronghold of my life—
of whom shall I be afraid?...
One thing I ask of the LORD,
this only do I seek:
that I may dwell in the house of the LORD
all the days of my life,
to gaze on the beauty of the LORD
and to seek him in his temple.
For in the day of trouble
he will keep me safe in his dwelling;
he will hide me in the shelter of his sacred tent
and set me high upon a rock.

PSALM 27:1, 4–5 NIV

Grasp the fact that God is for you—let this certainty
make its impact on you in relation to what
you are up against at this very moment; and you will find in
thus knowing God as your sovereign protector,
irrevocably committed to you in the covenant of grace,
both freedom from fear and new strength for the fight.

J. I. PACKER

The LORD is my rock, my fortress and my deliverer;
my God is my rock, in whom I take refuge,
my shield and the horn of my salvation, my stronghold.

PSALM 18:2–3 NIV

What can harm us when everything must first touch God whose presence surrounds us?

My Help

I will lift up mine eyes unto the hills,
from whence cometh my help.
My help cometh from the LORD,
which made heaven and earth.
He will not suffer thy foot to be moved:
he that keepeth thee will not slumber.
Behold, he that keepeth Israel
shall neither slumber nor sleep.
The LORD is thy keeper:
the LORD is thy shade upon thy right hand.
The sun shall not smite thee by day,
nor the moon by night.
The LORD shall preserve thee from all evil:
he shall preserve thy soul.
The LORD shall preserve thy going out and thy coming in
from this time forth, and even for evermore.

PSALM 121:1–8 KJV

We may not all reach God's ideal for us,
but with His help we may move in that direction day by day
as we relate every detail of our lives to Him.

CAROL GISH

We have a Father in heaven who is almighty,
who loves His children as He loves His only-begotten Son,
and whose very joy and delight it is to [comfort] and help them
at all times and under all circumstances.

GEORGE MUELLER

God makes our lives a medley of joy and tears,
hope and help, love and encouragement.

COMFORT SWEET

God comforts. He lays His right hand on the wounded soul...
and He says, as if that one were the only soul in all the universe:
O greatly beloved, fear not: peace be unto you.

AMY CARMICHAEL

There is a place of comfort sweet
Near to the heart of God,
A place where we our Savior meet,
Near to the heart of God.
O Jesus, blest Redeemer,
Sent from the heart of God,
Hold us who wait before Thee
Near to the heart of God.

CLELAND B. MCAFEE

Let the beloved of the Lord rest secure in him,
for he shields him all day long,
and the one the Lord loves rests between his shoulders.

DEUTERONOMY 33:12 NIV

You will never find Jesus so precious as
when the world is one vast, howling wilderness.
Then He is like a rose blooming in the midst of the desolation,
a rock rising above the storm.

ROBERT MURRAY M'CHEYNE

The LORD is my light and my salvation; whom shall I fear?

PSALM 27:1 KJV

Overcoming

Christ desires to be with you in whatever crisis
you may find yourself. Call upon His name.
See if He will not do as He promised He would.
He will not make your problems go away, but He will
give you the power to deal with and overcome them....
Suffering is endurable if we do not have to bear it alone;
and the more compassionate the Presence,
the less acute the pain.

Billy Graham

He did not say, "You will never have a rough passage,
you will never be over-strained, you will never feel uncomfortable,"
but He did say, "You will never be overcome."

Julian of Norwich

Live today! Live fully each moment of today.
Trust God to let you work through this moment
and the next. He will give you all you need.
Don't skip over the painful or confusing moment—
even it has its important and rightful place in the day.

The world is full of suffering.
It is also full of the overcoming of it.

Helen Keller

I have told you these things, so that in me you may have peace. In this world you will have trouble. But take heart! I have overcome the world.

JOHN 16:33 NIV

All glory to God, who is able,
through his mighty power at work within us,
to accomplish infinitely more than we might ask or think.

EPHESIANS 3:20 NLT

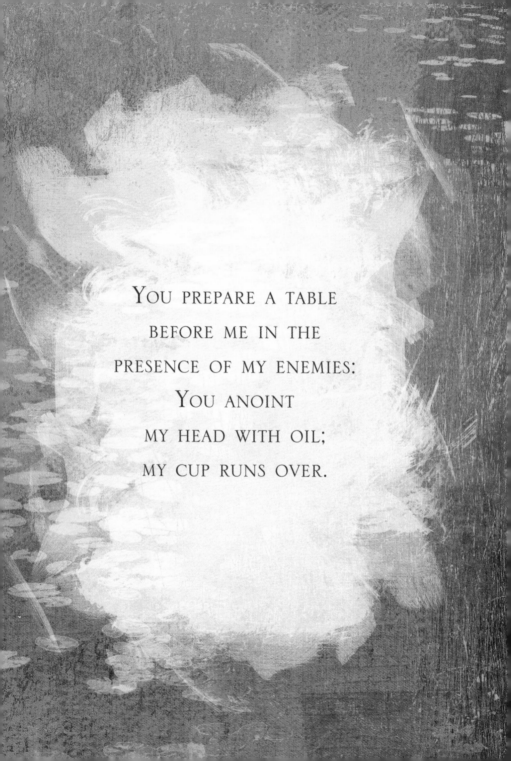

You prepare a table
before me in the
presence of my enemies:
You anoint
my head with oil;
my cup runs over.

Joy in the Journey

God is never in a hurry but spends years with those
He expects to greatly use. He never thinks
the days of preparation too long or too dull.

L. B. Cowman

God's training is for right now, not for some
mist-shrouded future. His purpose is for this minute,
not for something better down the road. His power
and His presence are available to you as you draw
your next breath, not for some great impending struggle.
This moment is the future for which you've been preparing!

Joni Eareckson Tada

Do not let your hearts be troubled. You believe in God;
believe also in me. My Father's house has many rooms;
if that were not so, would I have told you that I am
going there to prepare a place for you? And if I go
and prepare a place for you, I will come back and take you
to be with me that you also may be where I am.

John 14:1–3 niv

God may not provide us with a perfectly ordered life,
but what He does provide is Himself.

Judith Briles

*May the God of love and peace set your heart at rest
and speed you on your journey.*

RAYMOND OF PENYAFORT

ALL IS WELL

It's usually through our hard times, the unexpected
and not-according-to-plan times, that we experience God
in more intimate ways. We discover an unquenchable longing
to know Him more. It's a passion that isn't concerned
that life fall within certain predictable lines,
but a passion that pursues God and knows He is
relentless in His pursuit of each one of us.

WENDY MOORE

A living, loving God can and does make His presence felt,
can and does speak to us in the silence of our hearts,
can and does warm and caress us till we no longer doubt
that He is near, that He is here.

BRENNAN MANNING

If one is joyful, it means that one is faithfully
living for God, and that nothing else counts;
and if one gives joy to others one is doing God's work.
With joy without and joy within, all is well.

JANET ERSKINE STUART

Before me, even as behind,
God is, and all is well.

JOHN GREENLEAF WHITTIER

Lord, you have been our dwelling place throughout all generations.
Before the mountains were born or you brought forth the earth
and the world, from everlasting to everlasting you are God.

PSALM 90:1–2 NIV

DIVINE ROMANCE

To fall in love with God is the greatest of all romances—
to seek Him the greatest of all adventures,
to find Him the greatest human achievement.

AUGUSTINE

In the morning let our hearts gaze upon
God's love...and in the beauty of that vision,
let us go forth to meet the day.

ROY LESSIN

God did not tell us to follow Him
because He needed our help, but because He knew
that loving Him would make us whole.

IRENAEUS

Look deep within yourself and recognize what brings life
and grace into your heart. It is this that can be shared
with those around you. You are loved by God.
This is an inspiration to love.

CHRISTOPHER DE VINCK

The reason we can dare to risk loving others is that
"God has for Christ's sake loved us." Think of it!
We are loved eternally, totally, individually, unreservedly!
Nothing can take God's love away.

GLORIA GAITHER

For GOD is sheer beauty, all-generous in love, loyal always and ever.

PSALM 100:5 MSG

MIGHTY TO KEEP

God, who is our dwelling place, is also our fortress.
It can only mean one thing, and that is, that if we will
but live in our dwelling place, we shall be perfectly
safe and secure from every assault.

HANNAH WHITALL SMITH

God is adequate as our keeper....
Your faith will not fail while God sustains it;
you are not strong enough to fall away
while God is resolved to hold you.

J. I. PACKER

God of the years that lie behind us,
Lord of the years that stretch before,
Weaver of all the ties that bind us,
Keeper and King of the open door:
All through the seasons of sowing and reaping,
All through the harvest of song and tears,
Hold us close in Your tender keeping,
In Your arms let us dwell secure.

God stands fast as your rock, steadfast
as your safeguard, sleepless as your watcher,
valiant as your champion.

CHARLES H. SPURGEON

He who dwells in the shelter of the Most High will abide
in the shadow of the Almighty. I will say to the LORD,
"My refuge and my fortress, my God, in whom I trust."

PSALM 91:1–2 ESV

FULLY SATISFIED

O God, you are my God;
I earnestly search for you.
My soul thirsts for you;
my whole body longs for you
in this parched and weary land
where there is no water.
I have seen you in your sanctuary
and gazed upon your power and glory.
Your unfailing love is better than life itself....
I will praise you as long as I live.

PSALM 63:1–4 NLT

The Lord's chief desire is to reveal Himself to you and,
in order for Him to do that, He gives you abundant grace.
The Lord gives you the experience of enjoying His presence.
He touches you, and His touch is so delightful that,
more than ever, you are drawn inwardly to Him.

MADAME JEANNE GUYON

Like newborn babies, crave pure spiritual milk,
so that by it you may grow up in your salvation,
now that you have tasted that the Lord is good.

1 PETER 2:2–3 NIV

Genuine heart-hunger, accompanied by sincere
seeking after eternal values, does not go unrewarded.

JUSTINE KNIGHT

Only God can fully satisfy the hungry heart.
HUGH BLACK

Fill Me Up, Lord

When I am in solitude, the presence of God is so real
and so full that there is nothing else I want.
The people I love are with me in God's presence,
beyond the surface choppiness of all the stresses
that separate us as finite beings on this earth,
and I am able to experience our ultimate togetherness in God.
This experience is absolutely the only thing that
fills the longing of my heart.

RUTH HALEY BARTON

The LORD will guide you always;
he will satisfy your needs in a sun-scorched land
and will strengthen your frame.
You will be like a well-watered garden,
like a spring whose waters never fail.

ISAIAH 58:11 NIV

Prayer is to the spirit what breath is to the body.
We treat prayer as though it were the spice of life,
but the Bible prescribes it as a vital staple in our diet.

DAVID HUBBARD

The overflowing life does not just happen.
It is only as our own deep thirst is quenched,
only as we are filled ourselves, that we can be channels
through which His overflow reaches other lives.

GRACE STRICKER DAWSON

Our love to God arises out of our emptiness;
God's love to us out of His fullness.

HANNAH MORE

BLESSED ASSURANCE

So wait before the Lord. Wait in the stillness.
And in that stillness, assurance will come to you.
You will know that you are heard; you will know that
your Lord ponders the voice of your humble desires;
you will hear quiet words spoken to you yourself,
perhaps to your grateful surprise and refreshment.

AMY CARMICHAEL

Let us draw near to God with a sincere heart
and with the full assurance that faith brings,
having our hearts sprinkled
to cleanse us from a guilty conscience
and having our bodies washed with pure water.
Let us hold unswervingly to the hope we profess,
for he who promised is faithful.

HEBREWS 10:22–23 NIV

In those times I can't seem to find God,
I rest in the assurance He knows how to find me.

NEVA COYLE

Peace *with* God brings the peace *of* God.
It is a peace that settles our nerves, fills our mind,
floods our spirit, and in the midst of the uproar around us,
gives us the assurance that everything is all right.

BOB MUMFORD

*Be assured, if you walk with Him and look to Him
and expect help from Him, He will never fail you.*

GEORGE MUELLER

GOD KNOWS

God possesses infinite knowledge and an awareness
which is uniquely His. At all times,
even in the midst of any type of suffering,
I can realize that He knows, loves, watches, understands,
and more than that, He has a purpose.

BILLY GRAHAM

We do not know what we ought to pray for,
but the Spirit himself intercedes for us with groans
that words cannot express. And he
who searches our hearts knows the mind of the Spirit,
because the Spirit intercedes for the saints
in accordance with God's will.
And we know that in all things God works
for the good of those who love him,
who have been called according to his purpose.

ROMANS 8:26–28 NIV[†]

With God our trust can be abandoned, utterly free.
In Him are no limitations, no flaws, no weaknesses.
His judgment is perfect, His knowledge of us is perfect,
His love is perfect. God alone is trustworthy.

EUGENIA PRICE

If anyone loves God, he is known by God.

1 CORINTHIANS 8:3 ESV

Pour out your heart to God your Father.
He understands you better than you do.

ACCOMPLISHED IN HIM

The duties God requires of us are not in proportion
to the strength we possess in ourselves. Rather,
they are proportional to the resources available to us in Christ.
We do not have the ability in ourselves to accomplish
the least of God's tasks. This is a law of grace.
When we recognize it is impossible to perform a duty
in our own strength, we will discover
the secret of its accomplishment.

JOHN OWEN

God has a history of using the insignificant
to accomplish the impossible.

RICHARD EXLEY

Give yourself fully to Jesus—He will use you
to accomplish great things on the condition
that you believe much more in His love
than in your weakness.

MOTHER TERESA

Have courage for the great sorrows of life,
and patience for the small ones;
and when you have...accomplished your daily task,
go to sleep in peace. God is awake.

VICTOR HUGO

For God is the one who provides seed for the farmer and then bread to eat.
In the same way, he will provide and increase your resources
and then produce a great harvest of generosity in you.

2 CORINTHIANS 9:10 NLT

My Provider

Knowing God is putting your trust in Him.
Trust that He loves you and will provide
for your every need. When we know God,
we know Him like a personal friend. We have no reason
to be scared of God. God is for us!
He will never leave us. Having "fear" of the Lord
is the same as having "deepest respect."
Because of who He is we have every reason
to feel respect for Him and show it
in the way that we live. We no longer fear the unknown,
fear the future, or fear our circumstances.

TOM RICHARDS

You can trust God right now to supply all your
needs for today. And if your needs are more tomorrow,
His supply will be greater also.

God's gifts make us truly wealthy.
His loving supply never shall leave us wanting.

BECKY LAIRD

Each of us may be sure that if God sends us on stony paths
He will provide us with strong shoes, and He will not send us out
on any journey for which He does not equip us well.

ALEXANDER MACLAREN

*God will generously provide all you need. Then you will always have
everything you need and plenty left over to share with others.*

2 CORINTHIANS 9:8 NLT

PREPARED FOR WONDER

We are so preciously loved by God that we
cannot even comprehend it. No created being can ever
know how much and how sweetly and tenderly
God loves them. It is only with the help of His grace that
we are able to persevere in spiritual contemplation
with endless wonder at His high, surpassing, immeasurable love
which our Lord in His goodness has for us.

JULIAN OF NORWICH

By Jesus' gracious, kindly Spirit, He moves
in our lives, sharing His very own life with us....
He introduces the exotic fruits of His own person
into the prepared soil of our hearts,
there they take root and flourish.

W. PHILIP KELLER

The reflective life is a way of living
that prepares the heart so that something of
eternal significance can be planted there.
Who knows what seeds may come to us,
or what harvest will come of them.

KEN GIRE

For God Himself works in our souls, in their deepest depths,
taking increasing control as we are progressively
willing to be prepared for His wonder.

THOMAS R. KELLY

Oh, how great is Your goodness, Which You have laid up for those who fear You, Which You have prepared for those who trust in You.

PSALM 31:19

PATTERN OF BLESSINGS

Taken separately, the experiences of life can work harm
and not good. Taken together, they make
a pattern of blessing and strength the like of which
the world does not know.

V. RAYMOND EDMAN

Lift up your eyes. Your heavenly Father waits to bless you—
in inconceivable ways to make your life
what you never dreamed it could be.

ANNE ORTLUND

It isn't raining rain for you. It's raining blessing.
For, if you will but believe your Father's Word,
under that beating rain are springing up spiritual flowers
of such fragrance and beauty as never before
grew in that stormless, unchastened life of yours.

Whether we are poets or parents or teachers
or artists or gardeners, we must start
where we are and use what we have.
In the process of creation and relationship,
what seems mundane and trivial may
show itself to be holy, precious, part of a pattern.

LUCI SHAW

Isn't everything you have and everything you are sheer gifts from God?

1 CORINTHIANS 4:7 MSG

*God came to us because God wanted to join us on the road,
to listen to our story, and to help us realize that we are not walking
in circles but moving toward the house of peace and joy.*

HENRI J. M. NOUWEN

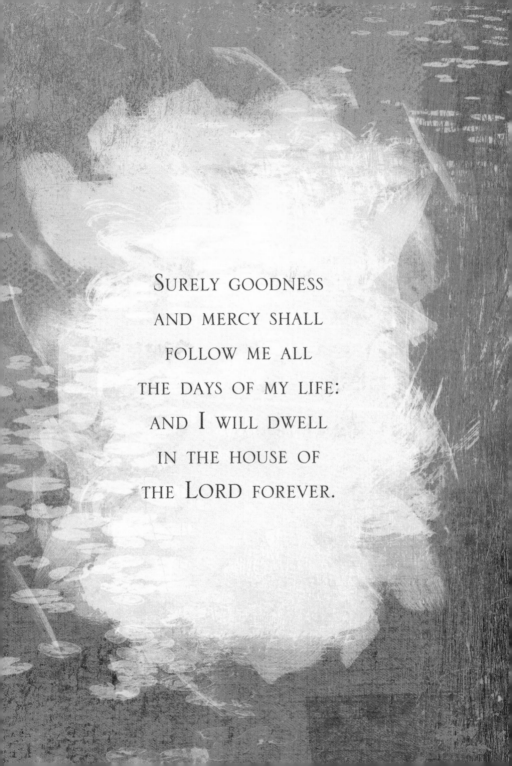

SURELY GOODNESS
AND MERCY SHALL
FOLLOW ME ALL
THE DAYS OF MY LIFE:
AND I WILL DWELL
IN THE HOUSE OF
THE LORD FOREVER.

THE GRANDEUR OF GOD

He writes in characters too grand
For our short sight to understand;
We catch but broken strokes, and try
To fathom all the mystery
Of withered hopes, of death, of life,
The endless war, the useless strife,—
But there, with larger, clearer sight,
We shall see this: His way was right.

JOHN OXENHAM

When God is about to do something great,
He starts with a difficulty.
When He is about to do something truly magnificent,
He starts with an impossibility.

ARMIN GESSWEIN

Take a moment to consider the awesome reality
that the God who spoke and created the universe is now
speaking to you. If Jesus could speak and raise the dead,
calm a storm...and heal the incurable, then what effect might
a word from Him have upon your life?

HENRY T. BLACKABY

Sing a new song to the LORD!...
Honor and majesty surround him;
strength and beauty fill his sanctuary.

PSALM 96:1, 6 NLT

The world is charged with the grandeur of God.

GERARD MANLEY HOPKINS

No More Tears

God washes the eyes by tears until
they can behold the invisible land
where tears shall come no more.

Henry Ward Beecher

I heard a loud voice from the throne saying,
"Look! God's dwelling place is now among the people
and he will dwell with them. They will be his people,
and God himself will be with them and be their God.
'He will wipe every tear from their eyes. There will be
no more death' or mourning or crying or pain, for the old
order of things has passed away." He who was seated
on the throne said, "I am making everything new!"

Revelation 21:3–6 niv

We can be assured of this: God, who knows all and sees all,
will set all things straight in the end. Even better,
He will dry every tear. In the meantime He mysteriously
takes our sorrows and uses them.

Richard J. Foster

Those who plant in tears
will harvest with shouts of joy.
They weep as they go to plant their seed,
but they sing as they return with the harvest.

Psalm 126:5–6 nlt

The Lord GOD will wipe tears away from all faces.

ISAIAH 25:8 NASB

Close to Him

That is God's call to us—simply to be people
who are content to live close to Him and to renew
the kind of life in which the closeness is felt and experienced.

Thomas Merton

God wants His children to establish
such a close relationship with Him that He becomes
a natural partner in all the experiences of life.

Gloria Gaither

The miracle of joy is this: It happens when there is
no apparent reason for it. Circumstances may call for despair.
Yet something different rouses itself inside us....
We remember God. We remember He is love.
We remember He is near.

Ruth Senter

It is good for me to draw near to God;
I have put my trust in the Lord God.

Psalm 73:28

God still draws near to us in the ordinary,
commonplace, everyday experiences and places....
He comes in surprising ways.

Henry Gariepy

Have confidence in God's mercy, for when you think He is
a long way from you, He is often quite near.

THOMAS À KEMPIS

HEAVEN

Heaven often seems distant and unknown,
but if He who made the road…is our guide,
we need not fear to lose the way.

HENRY VAN DYKE

Heaven will be the perfection we have always longed for.
It will be filled with health, vigor, virility, knowledge,
happiness, worship, love, and perfection.

BILLY GRAHAM

But God is so rich in mercy, and he loved us so much,
that even though we were dead because of our sins,
he gave us life when he raised Christ from the dead.
(It is only by God's grace that you have been saved!)
For he raised us from the dead along with Christ
and seated us with him in the heavenly realms
because we are united with Christ Jesus.

EPHESIANS 2:4–6 NLT

The God who holds the whole world
in His hands wraps Himself in the splendor
of the sun's light and walks among the clouds.

High King of heaven, my victory won,
May I reach heaven's joys, O bright heaven's Sun!
Heart of my own heart, whatever befall,
Still be my Vision, O Ruler of all.

ELEANOR HULL

You already know that God is everywhere.... And where God is, there is heaven—heaven! where His Majesty reigns in glory.

TERESA OF AVILA

ALWAYS THERE

We need never shout across the spaces
to an absent God. He is nearer than our own soul,
closer than our most secret thoughts.

A. W. TOZER

God is always present in the temple of your heart...
His home. And when you come in to meet Him there,
you find that it is the one place of deep satisfaction
where every longing is met.

Late have I loved You,
O beauty so ancient and so new.
Late have I loved You!
You were within me while I
have gone outside to seek You.
Unlovely myself, I rushed towards
all those lovely things You had made.
And always You were with me.

AUGUSTINE

I know the LORD is always with me.
I will not be shaken, for he is right beside me.
No wonder my heart is glad, and I rejoice.

PSALM 16:8–9 NLT

Tuck [this] thought into your heart today.
Treasure it. Your Father God cares about
your daily everythings that concern you.

KAY ARTHUR

Always be in a state of expectancy, and see that you leave room for God to come in as He likes.

OSWALD CHAMBERS

ETERNAL EXISTENCE

From the world we see, hear, and touch,
we behold inspired visions that reveal God's glory.
In the sun's light, we catch warm rays of grace
and glimpse His eternal design. In the birds' song,
we hear His voice and it reawakens our need of Him.
At the wind's touch, we feel His Spirit
and sense our eternal existence.

WENDY MOORE

Friendships, family ties, the companionship of little children...
the counterpoint of a Bach fugue or the melodic line
of a Beethoven sonata, the fluted note of bird song,
the glowing glory of a sunset:
the world is aflame with things of eternal moment.

E. MARGARET CLARKSON

I see nature once more playing endless
variations in design and beauty....
In such simple yet eloquent ways,
I am reminded that God is personal,
revealing Himself continuously in the finite.

Christ is the visible image of the invisible God....
Everything was created through him and for him.
He existed before anything else,
and he holds all creation together.

COLOSSIANS 1:15–17 NLT

To be with God, in whatever stage of being, under whatever conditions of existence, is to be in heaven.

DORA GREENWELL

A Safe Journey

God loves to look at us, and loves it
when we will look back at Him.
Even when we try to run away from our troubles...
God will find us, bless us, even
when we feel most alone, unsure.... God will
find a way to let us know that He is
with us *in this place*, wherever we are.

KATHLEEN NORRIS

Do not be afraid of the terrors of the night,
nor the arrow that flies in the day.
Do not dread the disease that stalks in darkness,
nor the disaster that strikes at midday....
If you make the LORD your refuge,
if you make the Most High your shelter,
no evil will conquer you....
For he will order his angels
to protect you wherever you go.
They will hold you up with their hands
so you won't even hurt your foot on a stone....
The LORD says, "I will rescue those who love me.
I will protect those who trust in my name."

PSALM 91:5–6, 9–12, 14 NLT

It is God to whom and with whom we travel,
and while He is the End of our journey,
He is also at every stopping place.

ELISABETH ELLIOT

There is no safer place to be than in the Father's hands.

The Goodness of God

All that is good, all that is true, all that is beautiful...
be it great or small, be it perfect or fragmentary,
natural as well as supernatural,
moral as well as material, comes from God.

JOHN HENRY NEWMAN

We walk without fear, full of hope and courage
and strength to do His will, waiting for the
endless good which He is always giving as fast as
He can get us able to take it in.

GEORGE MACDONALD

All we are and all we have is by the...love of God!
The goodness of God is infinitely more wonderful
than we will ever be able to comprehend.

A. W. TOZER

"The LORD is my portion," says my soul,
"therefore I will hope in him." The LORD is good to those
who wait for him, to the soul who seeks him.

LAMENTATIONS 3:24–25 ESV

Savor little glimpses of God's goodness and His majesty,
thankful for the gift of them: winding pathways through the woods,
a bright green canopy overhead, and dappled sunshine
falling all around, warm upon our faces.

Worship GOD if you want the best; worship opens doors to all his goodness.

PSALM 34:9 MSG

Steps of Faith

In the dark dreary nights, when the storm
is at its most fierce, the lighthouse burns bright
so the sailors can find their way home again.
In life the same light burns. This light is fueled with love,
faith, and hope. And through life's most fierce storms
these three burn their brightest so we also
can find our way home again.

God give me joy in the common things:
In the dawn that lures, the eve that sings...
In the springtime's spacious field of gold,
In the precious light by winter doled...
In the thought that life has love to spend,
In the faith that God's at journey's end.
God give me hope for each day that springs,
God give me joy in the common things!

Thomas Curtis Clark

Why should we live halfway up the hill
and swathed in the mists, when we
might have an unclouded sky and a radiant sun
over our heads if we would climb higher
and walk in the light of His face?

Alexander Maclaren

Faith goes up the stairs that love has made
and looks out the window which hope has opened.

Charles H. Spurgeon

Let love and faithfulness never leave you; bind them around your neck,
write them on the tablet of your heart.

PROVERBS 3:3 NIV

His Eternal Love

God, who is love—who is, if I may say it this way,
made out of love—simply cannot help but shed
blessing on blessing upon us. We do not need to beg,
for He simply cannot help it!

Hannah Whitall Smith

The Lord is like a father to his children,
tender and compassionate to those who fear him.
For he knows how weak we are;
he remembers we are only dust.
Our days on earth are like grass;
like wildflowers, we bloom and die.
The wind blows, and we are gone—
as though we had never been here.
But the love of the Lord remains forever....
The Lord has made the heavens his throne;
from there he rules over everything.

Psalm 103:13–17, 19 nlt

The kiss of eternal life, and the warm
embrace of God's Word, are so sweet,
and bring such pleasure, that you can never
become bored with them; you always want more.

Hildegard of Bingen

Love has its source in God,
for love is the very essence of His being.

Kay Arthur

With lavish hand Thou hast spread beauty across the world,
and I know love has planned it all.

KATHRYN BLACKBURN PECK

HIS DWELLING PLACE

How lovely are Your dwelling places, O LORD of hosts!
My soul longed and even yearned for the courts of the LORD;
my heart and my flesh sing for joy to the living God....
For a day in Your courts is better than a thousand outside.

PSALM 84:1–2, 10 NASB

We cannot kindle when we will
The fire that in the heart resides
The spirit bloweth and is still
In mystery our soul abides.

MATTHEW ARNOLD

Imagine yourself as a living house. God comes in to rebuild
that house.... You thought you were going to be made into
a decent little cottage: but He is building a palace.
He intends to come and live in it Himself.

C. S. LEWIS

You are living stones that God is building
into his spiritual temple. What's more,
you are his holy priests.

1 PETER 2:5 NLT

The soul is a temple, and God is silently building it
by night and by day. Precious thoughts are building it;
unselfish love is building it; all-penetrating faith is building it.

HENRY WARD BEECHER

If each moment is sacred—a time and place where we encounter God—
life itself is sacred.

Jean M. Blomquist

Everlasting Light

The sun will no more be your light by day,
nor will the brightness of the moon shine on you,
for the LORD will be your everlasting light,
and your God will be your glory. Your sun will never set again,
and your moon will wane no more; the LORD will be your
everlasting light, and your days of sorrow will end.

ISAIAH 60:19–20 NIV

Grace comes into the soul,
as the morning sun into the world; first a dawning, then a light;
and at last the sun in his full and excellent brightness.

THOMAS ADAMS

Light arises in the darkness for the upright;
He is gracious and compassionate and righteous.

PSALM 112:4 NASB

Trust! The way will open, the right issue will come,
the end will be peace, the cloud will be lifted,
and the light of eternal noonday shall shine at last.

L. B. COWMAN

God's touch...lights the world with color
and renews our hearts with life.

JANET L. SMITH

Those who have met God are not looking for something—
they have found it; they are not searching for light—
upon them the Light has already shined.

A.W. Tozer

Ellie Claire™ Gift & Paper Corp.
Minneapolis, MN 55337
www.ellieclaire.com

The Lord Is My Shepherd
© 2011 by Ellie Claire™ Gift & Paper Corp.

ISBN 978-1-60936-238-6

Compiled by Barbara Farmer
Cover and interior designed by Lisa and Jeff Franke

Printed in China